CLASSIC RIDES

CLASSIC

Corvettes

BY CLAIRE ROMAINE

Please visit our website, www.enslow.com. For a free color catalog of all our high-quality books, call toll free 1-800-398-2504 or fax 1-877-980-4454.

Library of Congress Cataloging-in-Publication Data

Names: Romaine, Claire, author.
Title: Classic Corvettes / Claire Romaine.
Description: New York : Enslow Publishing, 2021. | Series: Classic rides | Includes bibliographical references and index.
Identifiers: LCCN 2019041086 | ISBN 9781978517998 (paperback) | ISBN
  9781978518001 (6 pack) | ISBN 9781978518018 (library binding) | ISBN
  9781978518025 (ebook)
Subjects: LCSH: Corvette automobile—History—Juvenile literature.
Classification: LCC TL215.C6 R66 2021 | DDC 629.222/2—dc23
LC record available at https://lccn.loc.gov/2019041086

Published in 2021 by
Enslow Publishing
101 West 23rd Street, Suite #240
New York, NY 10011

Designer: Katelyn E. Reynolds
Editor: Therese Shea

Photo credits: Cover, p. 1 (left Corvette) Leena Robinson/Shutterstock.com; cover, p. 1 (middle Corvette) Emily C. McCormick/Shutterstock.com; cover, pp. 1 (right Corvette), 17 Tony Savino/Shutterstock.com; cover, pp. 1–32 (series chrome font) Mott Jordan/Shutterstock.com; cover, pp. 1–32 (series background) Sylvie Bouchard/Shutterstock.com; p. 4 Chesnot/Getty Images; p. 5 Scott Olson/Getty Images; p. 6 Los Angeles Examiner/USC Libraries/Corbis via Getty Images; pp. 7 (main), 11 National Motor Museum/Heritage Images/Getty Images; pp. 7 (inset), 9 (main), 22 Car Culture ® Collection/Getty Images Plus; p. 8 Bettmann/Getty Images; p. 9 (inset) © iStockphoto.com/Paul Pollock; p. 10 ISC Archives/CQ-Roll Call Group via Getty Images; pp. 12, 13 Jonny Bens/500px/Getty Images; p. 14 Bernard Cahier/Getty Images; p. 15 (main) Radu Bercan/Shutterstock.com; p. 15 (inset) Mindy Schauer/Digital First Media/Orange County Register via Getty Images; p. 16 Roger Dale Pleis/Shutterstock.com; p. 18 Grzegorz Czapski/Shutterstock.com; p. 19 Ralph Morse/The LIFE Picture Collection via Getty Images; p. 20 Charles01/Wikipedia.org; p. 23 Herranderssvensson/Wikipedia.org; p. 24 Ted Soqui/Corbis via Getty Images; p. 25 Doctorindy/Wikipedia.org; p. 26 Stephen Foskett/Sfoskett~commonswiki/Wikipedia.org; p. 27 David Cooper/Toronto Star via Getty Images; p. 28 Steve Lagreca/Shutterstock.com; p. 29 Patrick T. Fallon/Bloomberg via Getty Images.

Portions of this work were originally authored by Heather Moore Niver and published as *Corvettes*. All new material this edition authored by Claire Romaine.

Printed in the United States of America

Some of the images in this book illustrate individuals who are models. The depictions do not imply actual situations or events.

CPSIA compliance information: Batch #BS20ENS: For further information contact Enslow Publishing, New York, New York, at 1-800-398-2504.

Find us on

Contents

WORDS IN THE GLOSSARY APPEAR IN **BOLD** TYPE THE FIRST TIME THEY ARE USED IN THE TEXT.

A CLASSIC Car

Corvettes are classic cars—and not just older Corvettes. The word "classic" can mean "an example of excellence" or "the best of its kind." Corvettes have long been considered to be among the best of American sports cars. Even people who don't know much about cars have heard of Corvettes.

GET THE FACTS!

Chevrolet, sometimes called Chevy, is a car company that began in 1911 in Detroit, Michigan. Its founders were Louis Chevrolet and William C. Durant. Chevrolet became part of General Motors in 1918. The first Chevy car was the Series C Classic Six.

Corvettes are made by the Chevrolet division of General Motors (GM). They started out with only a two-speed **transmission** but became high-performance vehicles with cutting-edge **technology**. Learning about changes to the Corvette's **design** over the years is an **engineering** lesson for every car fan!

EVERY MODEL OF CORVETTE HAS FOUND FANS OVER THE YEARS. SOME LOVE THE ROUNDED OLD DESIGN. OTHERS PREFER THE SLEEK NEW CORVETTES.

THE BIRTH OF THE Corvette

In the 1950s, half of all cars sold to Americans were GM cars. However, none were like the British sports cars Americans wanted. In 1951, Harley Earl was in charge of design at GM. He started to plan a car to boost Chevrolet's image.

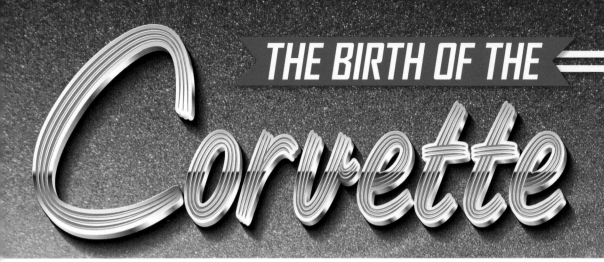

GET THE FACTS!

At first, the Corvette was only supposed to be displayed at GM's 1953 New York auto show, Motorama. Then, Chevrolet's chief engineer, Ed Cole, saw it. He knew right away people would buy it. GM started making plans to produce the Corvette.

THE 1953 CORVETTE HAD THE LOOK OF A EUROPEAN SPORTS CAR. GM CALLED IT THE "FIRST ALL-AMERICAN SPORTS CAR."

Earl worked on a new vehicle. He wanted it to be affordable but handle like a sports car. The secret design was called "Project Opel." It became the Corvette. Parts from other Chevy models were used to keep costs down. The body was made of lightweight **fiberglass**.

LIGHTWEIGHT FIBERGLASS

A DREAM Car

IN 1953, THE FIRST 300 CORVETTES WERE BUILT IN FLINT, MICHIGAN—BY HAND!

The first Corvette was so beautiful that it was called a "dream car." However, it wasn't as speedy as Harley Earl had hoped. It took 11.5 seconds to go from 0 to 60 miles (97 km) per hour. It also wasn't too affordable. Instead, it was the most expensive Chevrolet available at that time!

GET THE FACTS!

In 1953, Corvette owners didn't get to choose their Corvette's colors. All Corvettes were Polo White with black tops and red interiors. Also, the windows didn't roll down. To get fresh air while cruising, you had to stop to remove the windows!

However, car reviewers liked the fact that Corvettes could maintain high speeds on sharp curves. The front **suspension** was made so that the car would "stick" to the road when drivers went fast around tight bends.

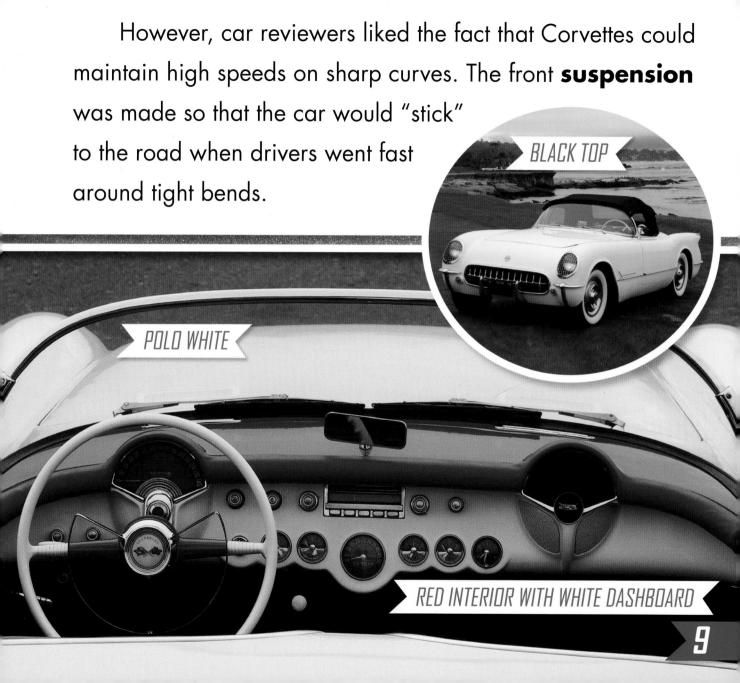

BLACK TOP

POLO WHITE

RED INTERIOR WITH WHITE DASHBOARD

THE C1s

ZORA ARKUS-DUNTOV

The first generation, or class, of Corvettes was produced from 1953 to 1962. The cars were called C1s. The 1954 Corvettes didn't change much from the 1953 model, but buyers could choose their car's color: Pennant Blue, Sportsman Red, Polo White, or black.

GET THE FACTS!

Zora Arkus-Duntov is called the father of the Corvette. Once a race car driver, he joined the Corvette team in 1953. Arkus-Duntov was daring and creative. His ideas kept new models of Corvettes rolling off the production line.

THIS IS A 1961 CORVETTE CONVERTIBLE, WHICH IS A CAR WITH A ROOF THAT CAN BE LOWERED OR REMOVED.

In 1955, engineer Zora Arkus-Duntov put an eight-**cylinder**, or V-8, engine under the hood. The Corvette's **horsepower** increased from 150 to 195. A four-speed transmission was first offered in 1957. Continued improvements included an even larger V-8 in 1962, which helped C1 Corvettes produce between 250 and 340 horsepower!

THE C2s

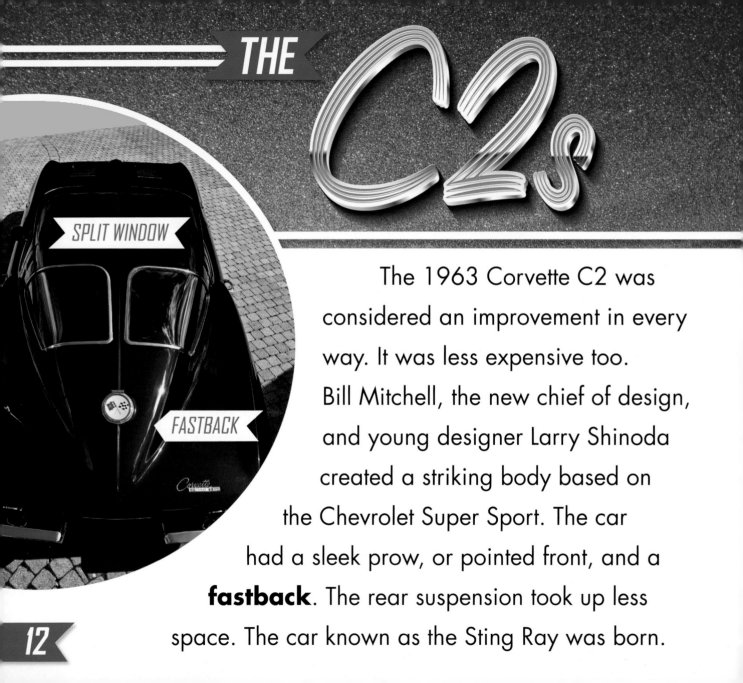

SPLIT WINDOW

FASTBACK

The 1963 Corvette C2 was considered an improvement in every way. It was less expensive too. Bill Mitchell, the new chief of design, and young designer Larry Shinoda created a striking body based on the Chevrolet Super Sport. The car had a sleek prow, or pointed front, and a **fastback**. The rear suspension took up less space. The car known as the Sting Ray was born.

Zora Arkus-Duntov summed up his feelings about the car: "For the first time I now have a Corvette I can be proud to drive in Europe."

THE LOOK OF THE 1963 CORVETTE WAS BASED ON A RACE CAR'S DESIGN.

PROW

13

By 1964, the split-window design was gone. However, engine size and power increased in C2s. In 1964, drivers could choose a 365-horsepower engine. In 1965, a large, or big-block, V-8 engine offered up to 425 horsepower. The 1966 model had an even bigger engine. It was 427 cubic inches (7 L). The top engine for the 1967 Corvette was the L88. It gave the car more than 500 horsepower!

Many agree the 1967 Sting Ray is the best Corvette. In 2013, one with an L88 engine sold for $3.4 million!

1963 CORVETTE HOOD EMBLEM

THE C3s

T-TOP

   The third generation of Corvettes, the C3s, were produced from 1968 to 1982. This was the longest-running Corvette generation. The cars were based on a car called the Mako Shark II. It had a new shape and finer details. The coupe's roof, called a T-top, had removable panels. The older transmissions were replaced with GM's new three-speed Turbo Hydra-Matic.

GET THE FACTS!

The Sting Ray name wasn't retired completely. In 1969, it returned, but it was spelled as one word, Stingray. Bill Mitchell had used the one-word name for his 1959–1960 race car. The name was used until 1977 and came back again in 2013.

In 1978, the Corvette celebrated its 25th **anniversary** with two special models: a Silver Anniversary edition and a limited-edition replica, or copy, of the pace car for the Indianapolis 500 race.

ONE OF THE SPECIAL EDITION CORVETTES WAS MADE TO LOOK LIKE THE 1978 INDIANAPOLIS 500 PACE CAR. THE PACE CAR LEADS RACERS AROUND THE TRACK TO WARM UP THEIR ENGINES.

REAR SPOILER

OFFICIAL PACE CAR
62nd ANNUAL INDIANAPOLIS 500 MILE RACE
MAY 28, 1978

FRONT SPOILER

THE ASTRONAUTS'
Car

HIDDEN HEADLIGHTS

Beginning in the 1950s, Americans were filled with excitement about the space program. Alan Shepard, one of the first group of American astronauts, loved fast cars. He drove a 1957 Corvette when he joined the space program in 1959.

GET THE FACTS!

The *Apollo 12* crew members drove matching 1969 Corvette coupes. Charles "Pete" Conrad Jr., Richard Gordon Jr., and Alan Bean decided on a special design. The cars were gold with black "wings" and featured red, white, and blue logos.

The Chevrolet team created a special program for astronauts. Each was allowed to drive a new car for a year for $1. Shepard and astronaut Gus Grissom had a friendly competition fixing up their Corvettes and making them perform better. These high-flying astronauts were used to speedy vehicles!

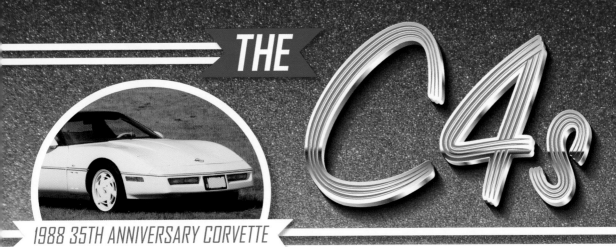

THE C4s

Chevrolet skipped the 1983 model year for Corvettes to allow for a complete redesign of the fourth-generation Corvettes, the C4s. The 1984 Corvette was very different from the 1982 model. The inside was roomier, and the instrument display looked more modern. T-top roofs were replaced by one piece, which could be removed with a wrench.

It was also much more **aerodynamic**, allowing for faster speeds. It could go from 0 to 60 miles (97 km) per hour in 6.7 seconds! Chevrolet perfected the C4s until their last year, 1996.

CORVETTE PACE CARS IN THE INDIANAPOLIS 500

- 1978 CHEVROLET CORVETTE
- 1986 CHEVROLET CORVETTE
- 1995 CHEVROLET CORVETTE
- 1998 CHEVROLET CORVETTE
- 2002 CHEVROLET CORVETTE
- 2004 CHEVROLET CORVETTE C5
- 2005 CHEVROLET CORVETTE C6
- 2006 CHEVROLET CORVETTE Z06
- 2007 CHEVROLET CORVETTE CONVERTIBLE
- 2008 CHEVROLET CORVETTE Z06 E85
- 2012 CHEVROLET CORVETTE ZR18
- 2013 CHEVROLET CORVETTE STINGRAY
- 2015 CHEVROLET CORVETTE Z06
- 2017 CHEVROLET CORVETTE GRAND SPORT
- 2018 CHEVROLET CORVETTE ZR1
- 2019 CHEVROLET CORVETTE GRAND SPORT

GET THE FACTS!

A powerful car like the ZR-1 has to have safety features, just like other cars. The 1990 model included a driver's side airbag and a security system. The ZR-1 had better **antilock brakes** than earlier Corvettes as well.

One of the standouts of the C4 generation of Corvettes was the exciting ZR-1, which became available in 1990. Nicknamed "King of the Hill," the ZR-1 had a V-8 that boasted a jaw-dropping 375 horsepower. *Motor Trend* magazine found that the ZR-1 could zip from 0 to 60 miles (97 km) per hour in 4.71 seconds! Such speed was only possible when the driver set a dashboard key to "full power."

LT5 ENGINE OF A C4 ZR-1

CAR AND DRIVER MAGAZINE SAID THE ZR-1 WAS "THE BEST THING YET SEEN FROM AN AMERICAN MANUFACTURER." AT TOP SPEED IT COULD DRIVE ¼ MILE (402 M) IN 13.4 SECONDS.

The ZR-1 wasn't just about speed, though. It had an improved sound system and was more comfortable.

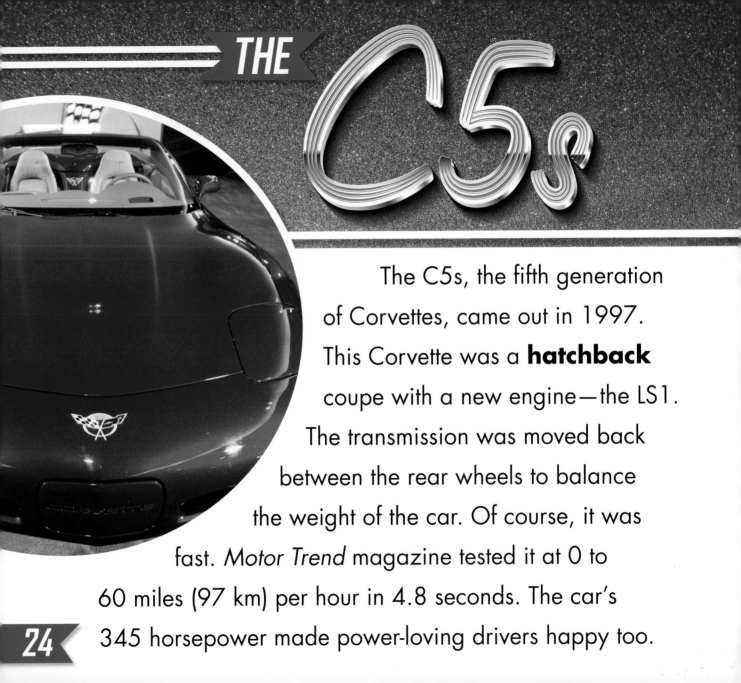

THE C5s

The C5s, the fifth generation of Corvettes, came out in 1997. This Corvette was a **hatchback** coupe with a new engine—the LS1. The transmission was moved back between the rear wheels to balance the weight of the car. Of course, it was fast. *Motor Trend* magazine tested it at 0 to 60 miles (97 km) per hour in 4.8 seconds. The car's 345 horsepower made power-loving drivers happy too.

GET THE FACTS!

Celebrating 50 years of Corvettes was a big deal to Chevrolet. To mark this, the 2003 models included a special edition Corvette in a deep red with a clay-colored interior. Special 50th anniversary markers were featured throughout.

In 2001, the Z06 was introduced with a top speed of more than 170 miles (274 km) per hour!

IN 2002, THE 50TH ANNIVERSARY SPECIAL EDITION CORVETTE WAS CHOSEN AS THE INDIANAPOLIS 500 PACE CAR, THE FIFTH TIME FOR A CORVETTE.

TOP SPEED—160 MILES (257 KM) PER HOUR

THE C6s

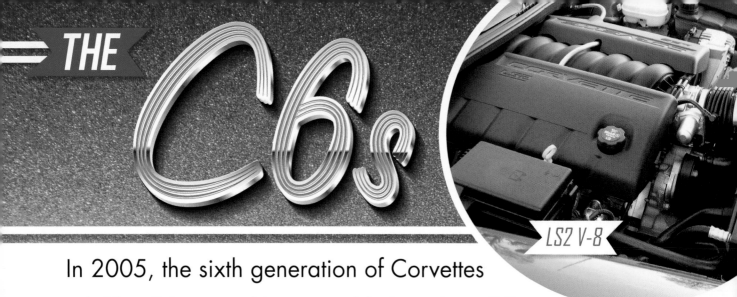

LS2 V-8

In 2005, the sixth generation of Corvettes arrived. The C6s were leaner and lighter than C5s. Headlights were no longer hidden as in the past generations. The 2005 model had an LS2 V-8 engine that produced 400 horsepower. It could zip from 0 to 60 miles (97 km) per hour in less than 4.2 seconds!

GET THE FACTS!

One model of the C6 generation was a special edition to celebrate Corvette's 60th anniversary. It was called the Corvette 427, after the measurements of its engine. It went from 0 to 60 miles (97 km) per hour in 3.9 seconds!

But designers weren't done yet. In 2009, the Corvette ZR1 came powered by a V-8 engine that produced 638 horsepower. It took the car to a top speed of 205 miles (330 km) per hour!

C7s AND BEYOND

In 2013, the C7 generation burst onto the scene with a new Stingray. A new version, or model, of the Z06 appeared in 2014 with an option for a supercharged LT4 V-8 engine with 650 horsepower! Chevrolet designers are always seeking to improve Corvettes yet keep them affordable. They use the latest technology to increase the thrills while maintaining a high level of safety.

The eighth generation of Corvettes began in 2020. Sports car fans can be certain this generation, too, will earn its place among the classic Corvettes!

GET THE FACTS!

Are you crazy about classic Corvettes? You can find them at classic car shows. You can also visit the National Corvette Museum in Bowling Green, Kentucky. This is also the location of the General Motors Corvette Assembly Plant.

EIGHT GENERATIONS OF CORVETTES

C1: 1953 – 1962   **C2:** 1963 – 1967   **C3:** 1968 – 1982   **C4:** 1984 – 1996

C5: 1997 – 2004   **C6:** 2005 – 2013   **C7:** 2014 – 2019   **C8:** 2020 – ?

THIS 2020 CORVETTE STINGRAY IS A LONG WAY FROM THE ORIGINAL TWO-SPEED SPORTS CAR OF THE EARLY 1950S!

Glossary

aerodynamic Having a shape that improves airflow around a car to increase its speed.

anniversary The yearly return of the date something special happened.

antilock brakes A braking system that allows a car to stop safely in wet or slippery conditions.

cylinder A tube-shaped space in an engine in which a piston is pushed by the pressure or force of a fluid.

design The plan or form of something.

engineering The use of science and math to build better objects.

fastback The back roof on a closed passenger car or truck that slopes in a long line toward the rear bumper.

fiberglass Glass fibers used in making various products.

hatchback A car design in which the trunk lid is replaced with a door that opens upward and usually includes the rear window.

horsepower A unit used to measure the power of an engine.

suspension A system of springs and other parts on a car that reduces the shaking and bumping caused by uneven surfaces.

technology A machine, piece of equipment, or process that is created by the latest scientific tools and methods.

transmission The system of gears that transmits power from a car's or truck's engine to the wheels.

FOR MORE INFORMATION

BOOKS

Aloian, Sam. *How a Car Is Made*. New York, NY: Gareth Stevens Publishing, 2016.

Kingston, Seth. *The History of Corvettes*. New York, NY: PowerKids Press, 2019.

Monnig, Alex. *Behind the Wheel of a Sports Car*. Mankato, MN: The Child's World, 2016.

WEBSITES

About Corvette
www.corvettemuseum.org/learn/about-corvette/
Read much more about each generation of Corvettes.

Chevrolet Motorsports
www.chevrolet.com/navigation/primarynavlink/vehicles.html
Find out what Chevys are on the racing scene.

Index